MAKING THE
MOST OF THE REST
OF YOUR LIFE

JOHN CHAPMAN

MAKING THE
MOST OF THE REST
OF YOUR LIFE

JOHN CHAPMAN

Making the Most of the Rest of Your Life
© Matthias Media 2007

Matthias Media
(St Matthias Press Ltd. ACN 067 558 365)
PO Box 225
Kingsford NSW 2032
Australia
Telephone: (02) 9663 1478; international: +61-2-9663-1478
Facsimile: (02) 9663 3265; international: +61-2-9663-3265
Email: info@matthiasmedia.com.au
Internet: www.matthiasmedia.com.au

Matthias Media (USA)
Telephone: 724 498 1668; international: +1-724-498-1668
Facsimile: 724 498 1658; international: +1-724-498-1658
Email: sales@matthiasmedia.com
Internet: www.matthiasmedia.com

ISBN 978 1 921068 76 8

Cover design and typesetting by Lankshear Design Pty Ltd.

DEDICATED TO
Margaret Orpwood and the late Michael Orpwood—
Christians, godly, hospitable friends.

Contents

Introduction

I HAVE ALREADY HAD MY 76TH BIRTHDAY, and I live in a retirement village on the outskirts of Sydney. Each year I seem to collect another specialist. They put the ailing parts back together again.

Life in a retirement village has been a new experience for me. The paper man comes every morning at 4.30 am and the ambulance at 9.15 am. Sometimes it brings people home, but not always. Your mortality presses in.

You may think it strange that I am writing about making the most of the rest of our lives. Humanly speaking, I don't have all that much left. The average male in Australia lives for 79 years. That doesn't leave me much time.

On the other hand, if there is life *after* death, if eternity is really eternity and I have the greater bulk of my life to look forward to, then that makes all the difference.

If there is life after death, is it possible to make the most of it? Is it possible to prepare for that life, or is it totally a matter of chance? These are the questions I want to address in this short book.

Jesus once told a story about a man who made detailed preparations for this life but neglected to make plans for the life after this one. God's view of this man is less than favourable.

Someone in the crowd said to him, "Teacher, tell my brother to divide the inheritance with me." But he said to him, "Man, who made me a judge or arbitrator over you?" And he said to them, "Take care, and be on your guard against all covetousness, for one's life does not consist in the abundance of his possessions." And he told them a parable, saying, "The land of a rich man produced plentifully, and he thought to himself, 'What shall I do, for I have nowhere to store my crops?' And he said, 'I will do this: I will tear down my barns and build larger ones, and there I will store all my grain and my goods. And I will say to my soul, Soul, you have ample goods laid up for many years; relax, eat, drink, be merry.' But God said to him, 'Fool! This night your soul is required of you, and the things you have prepared, whose will they be?' So is the one who lays up treasure for himself and is not rich toward God." (Luke 12:13-21)*

This man had lots of plans for this life but had totally neglected the life after this one. God labelled him a fool.

And he really is foolish. He makes three fundamental mistakes. Firstly, he mistakes himself for God. Did you notice how totally self-centred he is? "I will pull down the barns … I will say to myself …". He is the centre of his life. God is excluded. We know this because he is said to be "not rich toward God".

Secondly, he mistakes time for eternity. He thinks that he has "ample goods laid up for many years", but he doesn't have many years left. In fact, he doesn't have any years left.

His third mistake is to think that life is about making money and having things. But what good are all his

---

*In case you are not familiar with Bible references, 'Luke 12:13-21' means the book of Luke, chapter 12, verses 13-21.

possessions in the new life for which he is totally ill-equipped?

Not to plan for the inevitable is really foolish.

Planning for a long-term future

There are certain events which we can be sure about. One is death. I know that it is difficult to come to terms with this idea. When I was 21, I thought I was immortal. This idea lingered for quite a while. My observation is that most people continue to think like this, even when all the evidence is to the contrary. But the fact of the matter is that we will all die.

Last year, I went to a reunion of Moore College alumni for the enrolling years of 1956-7. I was shaken by how 'old' we had all grown. I made the fatal mistake of asking people how they were. I was treated to 'organ recital' after 'organ recital'. What surprised me was that everyone offered me a cure, even though it was very clear that none of the remedies were working!

The Bible has the view that all people will die, and that all people will survive the grave and live either *with* Christ or *without* him in eternity. I want to try and explore what real evidence we have for such a belief, if it is sustainable and, if so, how to prepare for that eternity.

1 | Life beyond the grave

SEVERAL YEARS AGO, I WAS WITH A GROUP of friends and we were discussing the possibility of life after death. One person said, "The trouble is that no-one has ever come back from the dead to tell us!"

This seems almost like an insoluble problem. Can we be sure that the concept of life after death isn't just wishful thinking? A bit like whistling in the dark to keep your spirits up?

After all, life here and now is solid, substantial and real. Life in the next age seems so 'ghostly'. The idea that we will all be sitting or lying around in the clouds with harps isn't all that appealing. However, the thought that there will be unlimited time and opportunity to give full scope to my potential—that is much more appealing!

Is 'life after death' an idea that humans have made up because we cannot do everything we want to in this life? Our potential is great and our time and opportunities are limited. Have we invented an afterlife to give ourselves hope?

I remember my mother at the age of 84 having extensive plans for the future. To have realized these, she would have needed to live until she was at least 250. When I suggested that she may not have enough time to achieve all her plans, she simply said, "You are a stupid person!" So I didn't pursue the matter further.

Is it wishful thinking? Is there any real evidence that there is life after death?

The fact of the matter is that someone has come back from the grave to tell us that there is life after death. That person is Jesus Christ.

The resurrection of Jesus Christ from the dead

During his lifetime, Jesus repeatedly told people that if they put their trust in him he would give them eternal life—a new life which begins now and goes on forever.[1]

Jesus also repeatedly told his disciples that he himself would pass through death and rise triumphant on the other side, although at the time they didn't understand what he was talking about.[2]

The Bible writers see the resurrection of Jesus Christ from the dead as the crowning glory of his ministry, and as the basis for his promise to offer people 'eternal life'. The significance of this great event is that Jesus has conquered death and is alive for ever more.

But did it really happen?

It seems fantastic to claim that Jesus came back to life again from the dead. Indeed it is, and we would want excellent evidence to believe it, since none of us were there to see for ourselves.

The leaders of the early church all claimed to have seen Jesus alive and well after his death and burial.

The Apostle Paul describes it like this:

> Now I would remind you, brothers, of the gospel I preached to you, which you received, in which you stand, and by which you are being saved, if you hold fast to the word I preached to you—unless you believed in vain.

> For I delivered to you as of first importance what I also received: that Christ died for our sins in accordance with the Scriptures, that he was buried, that he was raised on the third day in accordance with the Scriptures, and that he appeared to Cephas, then to the twelve. Then he appeared to more than five hundred brothers at one time, most of whom are still alive, though some have fallen asleep. Then he appeared to James, then to all the apostles. (1 Corinthians 15:1-7)

Please notice that within a decade or so of the death of Jesus, Paul is able to appeal to a wide group of people who claim to have seen Jesus alive after his death. It is as if he is saying, "You can ask any of the church people in Jerusalem. They all saw him."

All four Gospel writers—Matthew, Mark, Luke and John—record incidents where people saw and spoke with Jesus after his death. Luke has a very interesting account of Jesus appearing to the disciples:

> As they were talking about these things, Jesus himself stood among them, and said to them, "Peace to you!" But they were startled and frightened and thought they saw a spirit. And he said to them, "Why are you troubled, and why do doubts arise in your hearts? See my hands and my feet, that it is I myself. Touch me, and see. For a spirit does not have flesh and bones as you see that I have." And when he had said this, he showed them his hands and his feet. And while they still disbelieved for joy and were marveling, he said to them, "Have you anything here to eat?" They gave him a piece of broiled fish, and he took it and ate before them.
>
> Then he said to them, "These are my words that I spoke to you while I was still with you, that everything

written about me in the Law of Moses and the Prophets and the Psalms must be fulfilled." Then he opened their minds to understand the Scriptures, and said to them, "Thus it is written, that the Christ should suffer and on the third day rise from the dead, and that repentance and forgiveness of sins should be proclaimed in his name to all nations, beginning from Jerusalem. You are witnesses of these things. And behold, I am sending the promise of my Father upon you. But stay in the city until you are clothed with power from on high." (Luke 24:36-49)

Notice how Jesus is at pains to reassure them that it is really himself. He is not a ghost. He has a resurrection body. He could be touched and felt, and he ate some fish to assure them. He had a physical body and he was recognized. There was no mistake—it was Jesus himself.

John, in his Gospel, records an unexpected piece of evidence. Jesus appeared to his disciples, but Thomas was not present.

Now Thomas, one of the Twelve, called the Twin, was not with them when Jesus came. So the other disciples told him, "We have seen the Lord." But he said to them, "Unless I see in his hands the mark of the nails, and place my finger into the mark of the nails, and place my hand into his side, I will never believe."

Eight days later, his disciples were inside again, and Thomas was with them. Although the doors were locked, Jesus came and stood among them and said, "Peace be with you." Then he said to Thomas, "Put your finger here, and see my hands; and put out your hand, and place it in my side. Do not disbelieve, but believe." Thomas answered him, "My Lord and my God!" Jesus said to him, "Have you believed because you have seen me? Blessed are those who have not seen and yet have believed."

Now Jesus did many other signs in the presence of the disciples, which are not written in this book; but these are written so that you may believe that Jesus is the Christ, the Son of God, and that by believing you may have life in his name. (John 20:24-31)

This is a valuable piece of evidence. It explains how Thomas moved from doubt to belief. Thomas thinks he will never see Jesus again, so he declares, "Unless I poke my finger into the hole where the nail went in …". He would never have said this if he thought that he would actually have the chance to do it. When I was a little boy my father used to say, "John, if that ever happens I will walk from here to Bathurst on a cold winter's night on my hands without my pants on!" It was his way of saying, "It will never happen". Thomas is saying, "It will never happen". But it did.

No revision

As Christianity spread through the Apostles' preaching about the death and resurrection of the Lord Jesus Christ, it was the resurrection of Jesus which people found hard to believe. There is a very interesting event described in the Acts of the Apostles. The apostle Paul is in Athens, and he is asked to explain his teaching to the curious Athenians.

So Paul, standing in the midst of the Areopagus, said: "Men of Athens, I perceive that in every way you are very religious. For as I passed along and observed the objects of your worship, I found also an altar with this inscription, 'To the unknown god.' What therefore you worship as unknown, this I proclaim to you. The God who made the world and everything in it, being Lord of heaven and earth, does not live in temples made by man, nor is he served by human hands, as though he needed anything, since he himself gives to all mankind life and breath and everything. And he made from one man every nation of mankind to live on all the face of the earth, having determined allotted periods and the boundaries of their dwelling place, that they should seek God, in the hope that they might feel their way toward him and find him. Yet he is actually not far from each one of us, for

"'In him we live and move and have our being';

as even some of your own poets have said,

"'For we are indeed his offspring.'

Being then God's offspring, we ought not to think that the divine being is like gold or silver or stone, an image formed by the art and imagination of man. The times of ignorance God overlooked, but now he commands all people everywhere to repent, because he has fixed a day on which he will judge the world in righteousness by a man whom he has appointed; and of this he has given assurance to all by raising him from the dead."

Now when they heard of the resurrection of the dead, some mocked. But others said, "We will hear you again about this." So Paul went out from their midst. But some men joined him and believed, among whom also were Dionysius the Areopagite and a woman named Damaris and others with them. (Acts 17:22-34)

Did you notice the reaction when Paul spoke about the resurrection? People folded up in uncontrollable laughter. It was an impossible thing to believe. There is no doubt in my mind that the Apostles would have quietly removed the resurrection from their preaching had they not been convinced that they had seen Jesus alive.

It was not an easy or convenient message to preach. But they preached it. In fact, they were prepared to die for the fact that they had seen Jesus alive. Plenty of people will die for what they believe, but they will not die for what they know is a lie. The Apostles were prepared to die not simply because they *believed* that Jesus was alive, but because they had *seen him alive* after his death and burial.

The evidence that Jesus was dead and buried and that he came back to life as the conqueror of death is very good indeed. In this short space, we have touched on only some of the evidence.[3] To believe in the resurrection of Jesus is not at all unreasonable.

But what does it mean?

It is one thing to believe that Jesus came back to life from the dead, but it is important to realize the significance of this event.

He is God's promised king

Before Jesus was born, the Archangel Gabriel came to the Virgin Mary and told her that she would bear the Christ child. He described this soon-to-be-born child in the following way:

> "And behold, you will conceive in your womb and bear a son, and you shall call his name Jesus. He will be great and will be called the Son of the Most High. And the Lord God will give to him the throne of his father David, and he will reign over the house of Jacob forever, and of his kingdom there will be no end." (Luke 1:31-33)

We are told many things about Jesus here. One of them is that Jesus' reign would be without end.

Now we can be sure that if Jesus had died, and stayed dead, there was no way he could be God's promised king, whose kingdom would have no end. His reign would have ended with his death, as it has done with all kings before him and since. It was the resurrection of Jesus which assured the early Christians that Jesus really was God's king.

Jesus is alive now as God's king over all the world. We can relate to him as a living person. He hears us when we pray. He knows about our circumstances. He promises to guide us through life.

He has conquered sin and death

Death is a terrible curse. Last year one of my best friends died at the age of 61. Here at the retirement village, people die. There are some sad cases of people who have lost their spouses between selling their homes and moving into the village. It takes such a long time to develop good relationships and death laughs at them. You have a lifelong friendship, and then one morning you wake up and they just aren't there any more.

The resurrection of Jesus from the dead shows that he has beaten the effects of death. His resurrection body laughed at death. Someone, at last, has defeated it. The grave is not the end.

The Bible says that death is a consequence of our rebellion against God's rightful rule over our life. "The wages of sin is death" is the way one Bible writer expresses it.[4]

Jesus claimed that his death had a particular purpose. It was not simply a result of the jealousy of the Jewish authorities, and the weakness of Pontius Pilate. According to Jesus, his death was to take the punishment our sins deserve. He said that he had come to give his life as a ransom for us, to die instead of us, to pay the penalty for us.[5]

When Jesus rose from the dead, it was as if God was signing a paper saying, "Sins paid for in full!" We can be certain that Jesus' death was a sufficient sacrifice for our sins because he rose again from the dead.[6]

The result of sin is death. The result of sins being dealt with is resurrection.

He can take us through death

When you are in a new or threatening situation, it's always very reassuring to have someone with you who has been there before and knows the ropes.

Suppose I have been invited to the London club of a friend of mine. I am not a member. There is a doorman who checks that non-members are not admitted, and he says to me, "Excuse me sir. Are you a member here?" To which my friend says, "It's all right, Charles, he's with me". It is sufficient. It gets me in every time.

This is what Jesus has done through his death and resurrection. He is the first member of a new club, a whole new humanity. Jesus says to us, "I can take you into the new world of eternity. I am qualified. Because I have beaten sin and death, and been resurrected, you can be resurrected too. Trust me!"

Endnotes
1. John 3:15, 36
2. Mark 8:31-32, 9:9, 10:32-34

3. For a more detailed examination of the evidence, see Frank Morison's classic book *Who Moved the Stone?*, Authentic Media, Milton Keynes, 2006 (1930).
4. Romans 6:23
5. Mark 10:45
6. 1 Corinthians 15:16-20

2 | The new creation foretold

WHEN PEOPLE TALK ABOUT LIFE after death, they often speak of 'going to heaven'. This is understandable because the Bible speaks about heaven as God's dwelling place—as in "Our Father in heaven".

But when the Bible talks about what God is going to do in the future, and the eternity which people will spend with him, it doesn't talk about disembodied souls floating in heaven but resurrected bodies living in a 'new creation' that God will prepare for his people.

What does the Bible mean by a 'new creation'?

To answer that, we have to begin with the 'old creation' —that is, with this present world in which we live.

The Bible begins with a description of the way God intended this world to be. God creates a wonderful world, a world which he himself regards as "very good".[1] In the Garden of Eden, the man and the woman live together in perfect harmony with each other. They have charge of the garden and the animals. They are at peace with God. They have everything they need. It could be summed up with the phrase "Everything in the garden was lovely".

By the time we get to the end of chapter 3 of Genesis, all that has changed. The man and the woman are living in a strained relationship. Instead of loving harmony, they are competing with each other. And they are out of sorts with God. Instead of greeting him with happy anticipation, they run away from him and hide. They argue with God and blame him for their troubles.

Even the environment—the ground which produces their food—has become hostile to them. It produces thorns and thistles, and yields its fruit only by the sweat of the man's brow.

What has caused this terrible state?

The man and the woman rebelled against the good rule of God over them. They pushed him aside in an attempt to be gods themselves. Part of their punishment was to live in a world that is broken, frustrated, out of joint. Their world keeps crying out "All is not well".

The rest of the Bible tells the long story of how God is going to fix the problems of this 'out of joint' creation by bringing in a new creation, and reconciling people to himself so that they can be part of it.

THIS STORY OF RESTORATION AND salvation begins with God choosing one man (Abraham) and one nation (Israel) to be his own special people, as a kind of 'pilot project' for what he is eventually going to do in the whole world.

One of the key stages in God's plan for Israel was the appointment of a king. The king of Israel (also referred to as the 'anointed one' or 'Messiah') was meant to represent God in ruling and judging the people, and rescuing them from their enemies.

From its very beginning, however, in about 900 BC with King Saul, the story of the Israelite monarchy was a sorry saga. With rare exceptions,[2] after the reign of Kings David and Solomon, the kings of the Jews never lived up to expectations. They were every bit as rebellious as the

Israelites they were supposed to be leading. In fact, they were every bit as rebellious as Adam and Eve.

As the monarchy declined into more and more ungodliness, and the nation into more and more disaster, the prophets predicted that God would turn the situation around through a new, 'perfect' king or Messiah.

The prophet Isaiah foretold this in a wonderful poem about the new world which will be ushered in by the Messiah (or king), the ruler of God's world.

> There shall come forth a shoot from the stump of Jesse,
>   and a branch from his roots shall bear fruit.
> And the Spirit of the LORD shall rest upon him,
>   the Spirit of wisdom and understanding,
>   the Spirit of counsel and might,
>   the Spirit of knowledge and the fear of the LORD.
> And his delight shall be in the fear of the LORD.
> He shall not judge by what his eyes see,
>   or decide disputes by what his ears hear,
> but with righteousness he shall judge the poor,
>   and decide with equity for the meek of the earth;
> and he shall strike the earth with the rod of his mouth,
>   and with the breath of his lips he shall kill the wicked.
> Righteousness shall be the belt of his waist,
>   and faithfulness the belt of his loins.
> The wolf shall dwell with the lamb,
>   and the leopard shall lie down with the young goat,
> and the calf and the lion and the fattened calf together;
>   and a little child shall lead them.
> The cow and the bear shall graze;
>   their young shall lie down together;
>   and the lion shall eat straw like the ox.
> The nursing child shall play over the hole of the cobra,
>   and the weaned child shall put his hand on the adder's den.

They shall not hurt or destroy
 in all my holy mountain;
for the earth shall be full of the knowledge of the LORD
 as the waters cover the sea. (Isaiah 11:1-9)

This new king will rule with justice. He will not be able to have the wool pulled over his eyes. Bribery will be unknown in his reign.

He will, above all, bring in a whole new creation.

It will be like the present creation but with significant changes! The lion will eat straw with the ox, which is very good news for the ox. The child will play at the hole of the cobra. There will be no danger and no harm. My experience with little children is that great care needs to be taken at all times to see that they are not in danger. I read of two toddlers who climbed a ladder, fell into a water tank and drowned. Not so in the new creation.

In another poem Isaiah foresees that this coming king will bring about universal peace (a sort of a one-man United Nations). He beautifully describes the nations taking their weapons of war and reshaping them for use on the farm— "they shall beat their swords into plowshares, and their spears into pruning hooks".[3] What a terrific concept!

There is no doubt in Isaiah's mind that this will only be achieved by the Anointed One, the Messiah, and that it will involve a new creation:

"For behold, I create new heavens
 and a new earth,
and the former things shall not be remembered
 or come into mind.
But be glad and rejoice forever
 in that which I create;
for behold, I create Jerusalem to be a joy,
 and her people to be a gladness." (Isaiah 65:17-18)

And in Isaiah 66:22-23:

> "For as the new heavens and the new earth
>   that I make
> shall remain before me, says the LORD,
>   so shall your offspring and your name remain.
> From new moon to new moon,
>   and from Sabbath to Sabbath,
> all flesh shall come to worship before me,
>   declares the LORD."

According to Isaiah, God's new creation will contain a 'new Jerusalem' embracing people from all over the world. It will not be for Jews only, but open to everyone. By the time we get to the last book of the Bible, the writer of the Revelation describes it as follows:

> Then I saw a new heaven and a new earth, for the first heaven and the first earth had passed away, and the sea was no more. And I saw the holy city, new Jerusalem, coming down out of heaven from God, prepared as a bride adorned for her husband. And I heard a loud voice from the throne saying, "Behold, the dwelling place of God is with man. He will dwell with them, and they will be his people, and God himself will be with them as their God. He will wipe away every tear from their eyes, and death shall be no more, neither shall there be mourning, nor crying, nor pain anymore, for the former things have passed away."
>
> And he who was seated on the throne said, "Behold, I am making all things new." Also he said, "Write this down, for these words are trustworthy and true." And he said to me, "It is done! I am the Alpha and the Omega, the beginning and the end. To the thirsty I will give from the spring of the water of life without payment. The one who conquers will have this heritage, and I will be his

God and he will be my son. But as for the cowardly, the faithless, the detestable, as for murderers, the sexually immoral, sorcerers, idolaters, and all liars, their portion will be in the lake that burns with fire and sulfur, which is the second death." (Revelation 21:1-8)

And further in verses 22-27:

And I saw no temple in the city, for its temple is the Lord God the Almighty and the Lamb. And the city has no need of sun or moon to shine on it, for the glory of God gives it light, and its lamp is the Lamb. By its light will the nations walk, and the kings of the earth will bring their glory into it, and its gates will never be shut by day—and there will be no night there. They will bring into it the glory and the honor of the nations. But nothing unclean will ever enter it, nor anyone who does what is detestable or false, but only those who are written in the Lamb's book of life.

Is it possible for us to know, in reality, what it will be like in this new creation? All the accounts we have of it in the Bible are in poetic form (such as those above), and so we don't know a lot of the details.

We do know that it is not achieved by us, since it 'comes down from heaven'. We know that it is not a reformation but a transformation—it is something God does. We also know that it only happens through the kingly rule of the long-awaited Messiah, the Lord Jesus Christ, who is referred to in the passage above as 'the Lamb'.

But what will it be like?

ENDNOTES
1. Genesis 1:31.
2. Such as Josiah, who re-discovered the book of the law, and Hezekiah.
3. Isaiah 2:4.

3 | What will the new creation be like?

WE HAVE STARTED TO TELL THE STORY of how God is going to bring in a new creation which will last for all eternity. And we have seen that, according to the promises of the Old Testament prophets, the new creation will be brought in by the Messiah.

As the age of the New Testament dawns, it becomes clear that the long-awaited Messiah is none other than the Lord Jesus Christ ('Christ' is a Greek form of the Hebrew 'Messiah'). He is the one who finally brings salvation to rebellious humanity, and rules in God's new creation (or 'kingdom' as the New Testament often calls it).

As we watch Jesus throughout his earthly life, we get an inkling of what the new creation (or kingdom) will be like. As we see Jesus reversing the effects of human rebellion in this world, we catch a glimpse of the next world.

Let's take a quick 'walk' through Mark's Gospel and see for ourselves.

Jesus is its king (Mark 1:14-34)

The first time we meet Jesus in Mark's Gospel, he is walking beside the Sea of Galilee. There he sees Peter and Andrew casting a net into the sea. "Follow me", he commands.

Immediately they leave their nets and follow him. He goes a little further and finds James and John, who were also fishermen in partnership with their father. Jesus says the same thing to them. They leave everything and follow him.

Jesus behaves as king in his world, and his followers do just that. They follow.

In the incidents immediately following this, in the synagogue at Capernaum, Jesus continues to act with enormous authority. He speaks with such clarity and authority that people marvel at his words (Mark 1:22); he commands evil spirits and demons and they obey him (Mark 1:23-27); he heals diseases with ease (Mark 1:29-34).

In the new creation there will be no doubt who is in charge. The authority and rule that Jesus displayed on earth will be his in the new creation as well. He will be king. And Jesus' followers will offer to him their glad and willing obedience. They will see that the commands of their king are for their benefit, and for the benefit of others. It will be their chief delight to serve the one who has served them by dying as their 'ransom'.[1]

No more evil and sin (Mark 1:21-28)

There's something else we should notice about Jesus' actions at the Capernaum synagogue. His teaching is interrupted by a demon-possessed man who shouts out, "What have you to do with us, Jesus of Nazareth? Have you come to destroy us? I know who you are—the Holy One of God."

What happens next is astounding. Jesus commands the evil spirit to come out of the man. This takes place immediately. He exorcises the demons.

This is repeated again and again as we read through the

Gospel. Jesus meets sin and evil head on, and defeats them. Jesus is offended by every form of evil and sin. It is an affront to him (as it should be for us).

As Mark's Gospel progresses, we are told that Jesus' purpose in coming into the world was to deliver us all from the power which sin has over us (Mark 10:45). Jesus died on the cross to deal with sin; he died so that we could be forgiven.

Sin and evil will have no part in the new creation. Our disobedience to God has caused all the problems which have come upon the human race. If sin is not done away with, then the new creation will be no different to this flawed, broken creation, where people still prey on other people, where the weak and elderly are neglected, where minorities are ignored, and injustice and wickedness flourish everywhere like weeds in a garden.

But it will not be so in the new creation. What a brilliant world it will be! No paedophilia, no rape, no stealing, no fraud, no wars, no sin. What a world!

No more sickness (Mark 1:29-34)

When Jesus and his disciples left the synagogue, they came to the home of Simon Peter. His mother-in-law was sick with a fever. Jesus immediately healed her. At the end of the Sabbath, people brought all the diseased and demon-possessed people and he healed them all. None were incurable. He specialized in everything.

If you went to Sunday School or attended religious instruction at school you will be familiar with these actions of Jesus.

Wherever Jesus went, healing miracles followed as a

matter of course. It didn't seem to matter what the problem was—he had the solution. Lepers were healed (Mark 1:40-54). Paralysed limbs were enabled to function (Mark 2:1-12; 3:1-6). The demon-possessed were cured and became useful citizens again (Mark 5:1-20). The blind received their sight (Mark 10:46-52).

I begin each day with a handful of pills. I finish the day with another handful. I spend a lot of time in the waiting rooms of various specialists, who often tell me, "That is the best we can do for you!" My peers are the same. It is the lot of humankind, and especially the elderly. In the end, I will die from some bodily failure. There is no illness called 'old age'. Something will stop functioning.

But sickness will have no part in the new world. This is abundantly clear. See how this is described in the last book of the Bible:

> Then I saw a new heaven and a new earth, for the first heaven and the first earth had passed away, and the sea was no more. And I saw the holy city, new Jerusalem, coming down out of heaven from God, prepared as a bride adorned for her husband. And I heard a loud voice from the throne saying, "Behold, the dwelling place of God is with man. He will dwell with them, and they will be his people, and God himself will be with them as their God. He will wipe away every tear from their eyes, and death shall be no more, neither shall there be mourning, nor crying, nor pain anymore, for the former things have passed away."
>
> And he who was seated on the throne said, "Behold, I am making all things new." Also he said, "Write this down, for these words are trustworthy and true." (Revelation 21:1-5)

It is breathtaking! No more tears, nor mourning, nor pain.

Total forgiveness (Mark 2:1-12)

So far in Mark's Gospel, we have seen Jesus exercising extraordinary authority and performing remarkable miracles. But in the next incident, he does something even more remarkable.

Jesus has returned to Capernaum, having travelled through other villages in the region preaching the good news of the kingdom of God. So great was his fame that everyone gathered to hear his teaching. Four men who were carrying a paralysed man were unable to get into the building. They had total confidence that if they could only get their friend to Jesus, he would heal him. They climbed up on the roof, and made a hole big enough to lower their friend down into the room where Jesus was.

When Jesus saw them and took note of how much trust they had in him, he said to the man, "Son, your sins are forgiven".

This comes as a complete surprise. Up until now, Jesus has healed everyone who came to him. We are expecting Jesus to do the same for the paralysed man. But he doesn't. He forgives his sins instead.

Do you think the paralysed man was happy at this news? He wanted to walk. He wanted to become a useful citizen again. He was sick of begging and being dependent on others to help him. He felt within himself that Jesus could heal him (and he was right). Jesus could heal him, like he had healed all the others, but Jesus chooses not to do so. Something more important was at stake.

Without forgiveness, there is no way the man could be right with God. Without forgiveness, the man would not know what it was to have God guide him through life and he would not be able to spend eternity with God after this life. Jesus recognized the greater need, and he met that need before he dealt with the man's paralysis.

On hearing Jesus' words to the man, the religious experts who were present said to themselves "Who does he think he is? Only God can forgive sins."

Jesus knew what they were thinking (which is slightly spooky) and so he said to them, "Which is easier, to say to the paralysed man, 'Your sins are forgiven', or 'Rise up and walk?'"

The answer, of course, is that it is much easier to say "Your sins are forgiven" because no-one will know if you have the power to do that or not. However, the moment you say to the paralysed man "Rise up and walk", everyone will know at once if you can do it or not!

Jesus continues: "But that you may know that the Son of Man has authority on earth to forgive sins … I say to you, rise, pick up your bed, and go home". And in front of everyone, the man rises to his feet, hoists his bed, and walks off home.

This story has led me to believe that nothing is more important than being forgiven. Do you think that if you had the power to heal the sick instantaneously with a word, you would bother about their forgiveness before you healed them? I'm sure I wouldn't. I would heal them straight away. I'm sure I would say something like, "We can deal with their sins later". However, I have come to see that this is because I do not love people like Jesus does. He goes to the heart of their problem—an even deeper and more important problem than sickness.

In the new creation, everyone who is there will be a forgiven person. This is the special work that brought Jesus into the world. As we have already seen, Jesus came "to give his life as a ransom for many" (Mark 10:45). He did this on the cross, taking the punishment our sins deserved, so that we could be forgiven. He and he alone can say to each one of us, "Your sins are forgiven". Because Jesus died in our place, as our substitute, we can know forgiveness. We can be right with God.

This is the status of all the members in the new creation. Because they are all forgiven themselves, they will know how to forgive and accept others. It will be a wonderful world. One to be longed for!

Satan will be totally overpowered (Mark 3:20-30)

The evil of our world horrifies us. Political leaders have people murdered because they do not agree with them. They squander wealth while their people starve. They teach children to kill as if it were a game.

Evil is real and alive in our world, so much so that the existence of a devil or Satan—a malevolent centre of evil—makes perfect sense to many people.

Throughout Mark's Gospel so far, Jesus has been confronting the power of Satan and overpowering him. He has driven out demons and evil spirits with a single command. And so extraordinary was this display of power by Jesus, that some explanation was needed. The religious experts and teachers of the law wanted to know how he could do this. In fact, they said that Jesus himself was possessed by Beelzebub, the prince of the demons, and that this is where his power to toss out demons came from.

Jesus rebuffs this argument by saying, "How can Satan cast out Satan? If a kingdom is divided against itself, that kingdom cannot stand" (Mark 3:23-24). Such a state of affairs is impossible. Satan wouldn't destroy his own work.

No, something very different is happening says Jesus: "… no-one can enter a strong man's house and plunder his goods, unless he first binds the strong man. Then indeed he may plunder his house" (Mark 3:27).

In other words, evil and Satan may be strong, but Jesus is much stronger. He can easily defeat Satan, and release those who are captive to his power (and through his death and resurrection, this is exactly what Jesus did). Jesus is king, even over Satan and the supernatural world.

In the new creation, Satan will have no place. The terrible havoc he has wrought in God's creation will not be allowed to intrude into the new world.

No more natural disasters (Mark 4:35-40)

Of all the stories of the Lord Jesus, the stilling of the storm at sea is one of the most extraordinary.

Jesus has been teaching out of the back of a boat. And when evening comes, they travel over to the other side of the lake. A furious wind storm springs up and the disciples, many of whom are fishermen by trade, think that the end has come. "Don't you care if we perish?" they cry out to Jesus, who is taking a nap in the stern while all this is happening. Jesus simply commands the wind and the waves: "Peace! Be still!"

And immediately everything comes to a grinding halt. The wind stops howling; the waves stop heaving. There is a great calm. And the disciples are goggle-eyed. "Who then is this, that even wind and sea obey him?"

They knew that they were in the presence of a uniquely powerful person. If you want to test if you are that powerful, just take a trip across Sydney Harbour from Circular Quay to Manly on the ferry. When you pass the heads, where the swell is at its greatest, see if you can tell the waves what to do. Give it a try. My advice would be to do it quietly so that no-one will hear you.

Jesus is a person of very great power and authority. In fact, just before the storm-stilling incident, he had been teaching his disciples about this but they had not grasped it. Jesus chides them: "Why are you so afraid? Have you still no faith?" They had not grasped that Jesus really was king in this world.

What has this to do with the new creation?

As I pointed out in our last chapter, when humanity rebelled against God, part of our punishment was to live in a world that is broken, frustrated, and out of joint—a world of natural disasters.

In the new creation it will not be so. We will be in perfect harmony with the environment.

No more death (Mark 5:21-43)

Death is a taboo subject on the modern agenda. You can speak about anything in polite society except death. Most people I know live for pleasure and possessions. I think the way we deal with the inevitability of death, and the mockery it makes of our approach to life, is to ignore it in the hope that it will pass us by. If you wish to bring a dinner conversation to a crashing, grinding halt, remark to your hostess, "Have you given any thought to your death lately?" You probably won't be invited back, and you almost certainly will be struck off the Christmas card list!

That is what makes the next story in Mark's Gospel so significant.

A ruler of the synagogue, called Jairus, falls at Jesus' feet and pleads with him to heal his daughter, who is at the point of death. Jesus is happy to comply, but on the way he is delayed. Before he can get to the ruler's house, a message arrives with the news that the child has died, and that there is no further need for Jesus to come.

On hearing this, Jesus says to Jairus, "Do not fear, only believe".

When they arrive at the house, people are weeping and wailing loudly. "Why are you making a commotion and weeping?" Jesus asks. "The child is not dead but sleeping." They laugh at him, because they know the child really is dead.

Jesus puts them all out of the house, and goes into the child's room with her parents. He takes her by the hand and says, "Little girl, I say to you, arise." Immediately the twelve-year-old gets up and walks around with nothing the matter with her.

This is not the only such account in the Gospels. In the Gospel of Luke, we are told about the death of a widow's son in a village called Nain (Luke 7:11-16). In this case, the funeral procession is already on its way to the cemetery when Jesus stops the procession, raps on the casket and says, "Young man, I say to you, arise". To the astonishment of all, the dead man sits up in his coffin!

Since I was ordained, I have conducted hundreds of funeral services. It has never occurred to me to rap on the casket and say, "Young man, I say to you, arise"! There are enough difficulties at funerals without the minister being an idiot.

In the last book of the Bible, the author tells of a vision he has of the risen Lord Jesus. He is awestruck, and Jesus says to him:

"Fear not, I am the first and the last, and the living one. I died, and behold I am alive forevermore, and I have the keys of Death and Hades." (Revelation 1:17-18)

In the new creation there will be no death. There will be no trauma associated with sudden unexpected death. There will be no pain associated with the shattering of long-forged relationships.

Jesus, by his death and resurrection, has overcome death on our behalf.

Remember the way the last book of the Bible describes the new creation:

"He will wipe away every tear from their eyes, and death shall be no more, neither shall there be mourning, nor crying, nor pain anymore, for the former things have passed away." (Revelation 21:4)

No more hunger (Mark 6:30-43, 8:1-9)

This morning I searched Google under the word 'hunger'. There were 89,900 entries. The following quote is from a site called 'Freedom from Hunger':

- Freedom from Hunger concentrates its services on the world's poorest nations where, on average, 27% of children under 5 are moderately to severely under-weight, 10% are severely underweight, 8% of children under 5 are moderately to severely wasted, or seriously below weight for one's height, and an overwhelming 32% are moderately to severely stunted, or seriously below normal height for one's age.

- In the developing world, more than 1.2 billion people currently live below the international poverty line, earning less than $1 per day.
- Among this group of poor people, many have problems obtaining adequate, nutritious food for themselves and their families. As a result, 815 million people in the developing world are undernourished. They consume less than the minimum amount of calories essential for sound health and growth.[2]

For me, living in the rich Western world, these statistics are hard to take in. I don't ever remember being hungry, at least not in the way described above. I am not unaware that there is hunger in the world. I make a modest contribution through several agencies for the relief of hunger. I pray and long for a day when there will be such a distribution of the world's wealth that there will be no more hunger.

Two stories from Mark's Gospel give a glimpse of what such a world might be like.

Jesus is in the countryside and large crowds have followed him (5,000 in one story and 4,000 in another) because they are fascinated by his teaching. As the day draws on, it is apparent to the disciples that Jesus will have to stop so that people can go to neighbouring villages to get food. To their astonishment and alarm, Jesus tells *them* to feed the crowd. I have some sympathy for the disciples at this point. They have just been asked to throw together a meal for 5,000 people. "That would take eight months of a man's wages!" is their flabbergasted reply.

Jesus enquires as to what food is available. They tell him that they have managed to find five loaves and two fish. Jesus takes the loaves and fish, and blesses them, and begins to distribute them to the crowd. And everyone has more than enough to eat. In fact, Mark makes the observation that when they cleaned up afterwards, there were twelve basket loads of broken pieces of bread and fish.

In the new creation, there will be no hunger. None at all! There will be no thirst, no malnutrition, no starving children, no poverty.

Please don't misunderstand me. I don't think the poor should be neglected now because poverty will one day be no more. I think we should do as much as we can while longing for the coming of that day.

But thinking about the sheer extent of the poverty in our world, and the power of Jesus to feed the hungry, I long for the new creation!

No more insignificant people (Mark 10:13-16)

I remember reading somewhere that the two things we all need in order to function properly in life are security and significance. If this is true, we will all function extremely well in the new creation. The simple story related in Mark chapter 10 gives us a glimpse of this.

People were bringing their children to Jesus so that he would bless them. The disciples thought this improper and were trying to keep them away. Jesus is indignant, and says to them:

> "Let the children come to me; do not hinder them, for to such belongs the kingdom of God. Truly, I say to you, whoever does not receive the kingdom of God like a child shall not enter it." And he took them in his arms and blessed them, laying his hands on them. (Mark 10:14-16)

At the time of the Lord Jesus, children were very low on the social pecking order. Much as in Victorian England, children were to be seen and not heard. The idea that they were important to Jesus had not occurred to the disciples. But Jesus says that they are very important. In fact, he says that children are just the sort of people who will end up entering the kingdom of God. Just as children totally depend on their parents to care for and protect them, so the members of the kingdom will completely trust their king to protect and save and guide them. The only question is: does someone as powerful as the king of God's kingdom care about people like us? Are we significant to him? This story says that even the smallest and most insignificant child matters to Jesus.

The death of Jesus is the supreme proof of this. Once we realize that Jesus has loved us and died for us, we cannot doubt how much we matter to God. We may be well down the social pecking order in this world, but we are by no means insignificant to God. We matter to God. No-one is insignificant now, and neither will they be in the new creation.

THIS QUICK TOUR THROUGH PARTS of Mark's Gospel has given us a glimpse of what the new creation will be like; of what eternity will be like. It's a place where Jesus is king, and where under his rule there are no more tears or sorrow or disease or death; no more hunger or thirst or evil or sin.

It's a world that we could scarcely believe possible if not for Jesus. But Jesus entered our world, and showed us the kingdom in advance through his life, teaching, death and resurrection. Because of him, we can know what the new creation will be like, and we can be confident that it will come.

More than that, because of Jesus we yearn for it to come. In fact, when we pray "Your kingdom come" in the Lord's prayer, that's exactly what we're doing. We're expressing our desire that the new creation come.

I know that life in this present world seems so permanent, but it really is passing away. Of the eleven men I trained with in Teachers College in 1948-51, only five of us are left. Each time I go to another funeral I keep asking myself, "I wonder if I will be next?"

It is a real joy to know where your future lies. We *can* make the most of the rest of our lives.

ENDNOTES
1. Mark 10:45
2. Freedom from Hunger, 2006, viewed 11 May 2006, www.freedomfromhunger.org/info/.

4 | Who gets to go there?

I F THE NEW CREATION IS AS DESIRABLE as I have been suggesting, the burning question is: "Who will get to live in this new creation and, in particular, will I be part of it?"

To answer this properly, we need to backtrack a little and make sure we are clear about what is wrong with our present creation—because any observer of our world will see at a glance that all is not well.

We are at war with each other. I was 15 when the Second World War finished. (The Great War of 1914-1918 was supposed to be 'the war to end all wars'—but we are not so foolish as to say that again.) Since 1945, we have had wars in Northern Ireland, Israel and Palestine, Korea, Vietnam, Nicaragua, Ethiopia, East Timor, India, Pakistan, and the Congo, to name but some. Both the League of Nations and the United Nations have made valiant efforts to bring about peace. But have you ever asked, "Why do we have to work so hard at getting and keeping the peace? Why aren't we kind and conciliatory? Why don't we share the world's resources with each other? Is it because we are basically selfish?"

What can be seen on the world stage is also seen within our own nations and cities and suburbs and families. We find it hard to live with each other and not fight. In Western countries, roughly one in three marriages ends in divorce. No-one thinks that will happen when they marry!

Why do we hurt the people we love?

The obvious answer is that there is something very wrong with our world—or more to the point: there is something very wrong with us, with you and me.

The Bible explains what's wrong by sending us back to the very beginning, to the story of creation and of Adam and Eve. We looked at this in chapter 2 (you may remember), and we saw the wonderful picture Genesis paints of the good creation God made, and the pleasant and harmonious place humanity had within it.

However, this ideal state was soon disturbed. The man and the woman disobeyed God, and as a result almost everything changed. The man and the woman became a threat to each other. Their relationship with God was destroyed. The environment became hostile to them. The world, in other words, became as we know it today.

According to the Bible, the rebellion of Adam and Eve is typical of the way we all behave. The fact of the matter is that we don't *want* God to rule over us. We want to be independent. We feel it is our right to run our own lives as we choose. This rebellion is not always active. It can be expressed just as easily in passive indifference as in active defiance. But either way, the rebellion is real.

God's answer to our rebellion is to appoint a king—a king who will not only bring the rebellion to an end and crush any resistance, but who will provide an opportunity for rebels to turn back, to stop the rebellion, and to find forgiveness.

That king is God's own Son, Jesus Christ, whom he sent into our world.

Jesus lived a perfect life. He had no sin of his own. He always lived in obedience to God. That is why his life is so appealing.

However, even though he deserved no punishment and no death, he took the punishment which our sins deserved when he died on the cross. This was Jesus' mission, as he himself described it: "For even the Son of Man came not to be served but to serve, and to give his life as a ransom for many" (Mark 10:45).

This was at great cost to Jesus. Mark's Gospel describes the scene on the night before Jesus was betrayed, and handed over to the chief priests for trial:

> And they went to a place called Gethsemane. And he said to his disciples, "Sit here while I pray." And he took with him Peter and James and John, and began to be greatly distressed and troubled. And he said to them, "My soul is very sorrowful, even to death. Remain here and watch." And going a little farther, he fell on the ground and prayed that, if it were possible, the hour might pass from him. And he said, "Abba, Father, all things are possible for you. Remove this cup from me. Yet not what I will, but what you will." And he came and found them sleeping, and he said to Peter, "Simon, are you asleep? Could you not watch one hour? Watch and pray that you may not enter into temptation. The spirit indeed is willing, but the flesh is weak." And again he went away and prayed, saying the same words. And again he came and found them sleeping, for their eyes were very heavy, and they did not know what to answer him. And he came the third time and said to them, "Are you still sleeping and taking your rest? It is enough; the hour has come. The Son of Man is betrayed into the hands of sinners. Rise, let us be going; see, my betrayer is at hand." (Mark 14:32-42)

Here we see Jesus at prayer. He is on the eve of his crucifixion. He is about to take the sin of the world on himself. He will undergo God's wrath, the punishment for sin, on our behalf. That is "the cup" he is talking about— which is an Old Testament image of God's judgement and anger (see Isaiah 51:17; Jeremiah 25:15). No wonder Jesus is apprehensive; no wonder he is "greatly distressed and troubled". This is a massive thing he is about to do. We should never underestimate what Jesus did when he died for us.

The Bible says that Jesus, who knew no sin, became sin for us so we could be right with God (2 Corinthians 5:21). He died in my place so that I can be totally forgiven, and get right with God.

Was it necessary?

I remember a man saying to me one day, "What is all this hoo-hah about Jesus dying for me? My boys do naughty things. They say, 'Sorry' and I say, 'Let's forget it'. Why can't God be like me?"

But if God were to say about my sins, "Let's forget it", then he would be duty bound to say that to everyone else as well. To the thief, the murderer, and the sexual predator, he would have to say, "Let's forget it!" Can you imagine God saying to the relatives of the six million who perished in the Holocaust, "Let's forget it. It didn't really matter"? It is preposterous.

God is not careless about evil and sin (as we often are). If there is one thing the Bible is clear about, it is that God is passionately concerned about everything that happens in his world. He will see that justice is done. This is both good and bad news for us—good because truth will triumph, and bad because we are among the guilty. That is why forgiveness is so good.

Who gets to be part of the new creation?

It should be perfectly clear then that no-one who continues in rebellion against Jesus as the king will be able to be part of the new creation. If this were to happen, the new creation would end up just like the old creation. Nothing would have been achieved.

However, because Jesus died—and more than that, because he rose from the dead—he has achieved what God sent him to do. He has provided a way back for rebels, and he has been crowned king of the new creation, in which forgiven rebels have a home.

The Bible makes it clear that only those who have turned back (that is, 'repented') and been forgiven will take their place there. As we confess that we have been rebels and ask for forgiveness, God will readily give it. And as we wait for the new creation, we will want right now to live a new life under the kingship and direction of the Lord Jesus.

I guess the burning question is, "Will you be part of the new creation?" Only you can answer this. And how you answer it will determine just what you make of the rest of your life.

5 | Will you be in the new creation?

IN A PARABLE THAT JESUS ONCE TOLD about the kingdom of God, he made it pretty clear that not everyone will be part of the new creation:

> And again Jesus spoke to them in parables, saying, "The kingdom of heaven may be compared to a king who gave a wedding feast for his son, and sent his servants to call those who were invited to the wedding feast, but they would not come. Again he sent other servants, saying, 'Tell those who are invited, See, I have prepared my dinner, my oxen and my fat calves have been slaughtered, and everything is ready. Come to the wedding feast.' But they paid no attention and went off, one to his farm, another to his business, while the rest seized his servants, treated them shamefully, and killed them. The king was angry, and he sent his troops and destroyed those murderers and burned their city. Then he said to his servants, 'The wedding feast is ready, but those invited were not worthy. Go therefore to the main roads and invite to the wedding feast as many as you find.' And those servants went out into the roads and gathered all whom they found, both bad and good. So the wedding hall was filled with guests.
>
> "But when the king came in to look at the guests, he saw there a man who had no wedding garment. And he

said to him, 'Friend, how did you get in here without a wedding garment?' And he was speechless. Then the king said to the attendants, 'Bind him hand and foot and cast him into the outer darkness. In that place there will be weeping and gnashing of teeth.' For many are called, but few are chosen." (Matthew 22:1-14)

The idea of the kingdom of God (or of heaven) and the new creation are very closely linked, since the kingdom is ruled over by the king who also brings in the new creation. Did you notice that the kingdom is described as a celebration, the wedding of a king's son? The kingdom won't be like a long, boring church service. It will be a party!

Even so, it's a party that not everyone wants to be part of. In the first instance, the parable is about the rejection of Jesus as Messiah by his own people, the Jews. They refuse his invitation, and so the gospel goes out to all the other nations, who gladly receive him as their king.

However, the parable has a secondary meaning for us today. It extends a gracious invitation to all of us to join the kingdom of God. We are invited to recognize Jesus as our king and not push him away. We are challenged not to reject the invitation with feeble excuses; not to exclude ourselves from the kingdom and the new creation.

It is also important to notice that there is another person who gets ejected from the party. He has arrived at the wedding without wedding clothes. Now this is not because he couldn't afford decent clothes. It was the custom at the time of Jesus for the host at the wedding to provide elaborate costumes for people to wear. When you arrived, you would be given a costume, and provided with somewhere to change. In the parable, the man must have refused such a set of clothes. He simply arrived in his street clothes.

He represents people who want to be part of the kingdom but are not prepared to meet the fundamental requirement for entry. And for us, that requirement is simple: we need to turn to Jesus and put our trust in him for forgiveness. Some people won't accept this. They say something like, "If I'm not good enough as I am for God's kingdom, then I won't go". That is correct: they won't go. If we could make ourselves good enough for the kingdom of God, then there would have been no need for Jesus to come into our world and die for us.

It is a sad fact of life to realize that not everyone will be part of the new world. It makes it all the more urgent that we should take care that we *are* part of it.

Don't delay

Sometimes people think that there is no real urgency to take action. They think that there is plenty of time, and that they will deal with God's invitation later.

To delay is often fatal, for two reasons:

We don't know how long we have to live. Life is fragile. We could face judgement at any time. The fact of the matter is that we all die and none of us knows when. The wise person will be ready at all times.

The second reason why delay is foolish is that every time we say 'No' to Jesus we get better at saying 'No'. The more times you practise something, the better you get at it. Some people have been saying 'No' to Jesus for so long that they hardly have to think about it. It has become second-nature to them.

What a tragedy it would be to miss out on the best of the rest of your life!

What about my spouse?

Often when I have spoken about people's need to turn to Christ, someone has said to me, "My spouse has died and I don't think he or she will be in the new creation. So I'm not sure that I want to be where they will not be."

This is not a good reason to delay. We are not in a position to know what God's judgement has been on anyone. We may think we know, but in the end only God knows.

If your spouse could speak to you, would he or she urge you to be part of the new creation, or to reject Jesus and be excluded?

I'm not good enough

I have great sympathy with people who feel that they are not really good enough to be part of God's new world. The truth of the matter is that, left to our own devices, none of us *is* good enough!

However, the wonder of Jesus' death for us is that we can be totally forgiven. The new world will be peopled by forgiven sinners, just like us. It may be hard to believe that such complete and gracious forgiveness is possible; it certainly goes way beyond any forgiveness we might experience with other people. But God's word reassures us that God's forgiveness is complete and trustworthy. Look at this passage from the letter of 1 John in the New Testament:

> If we say we have no sin, we deceive ourselves, and the truth is not in us. If we confess our sins, he is faithful and just to forgive us our sins and to cleanse us from all unrighteousness. (1 John 1:8-9)

A prayer for us

Here is a prayer for you to pray if you would like to be sure that you will be part of God's great plan for the future:

Lord Jesus Christ,
I believe that you are king in God's world. I haven't been serving you as my king. From today onwards, I will try and serve you as best I can. Thank you for dying for me. Please forgive me and help me live with you as my king. Amen.

Where to now?

If you have prayed this prayer you have made a very good beginning. It won't be long before you will ask: "Well, what do I do next?"

The simple answer is: live out this prayer day by day, serving Jesus, obeying Jesus, and trusting Jesus for forgiveness.

It would take another book (or several books) to flesh out what this means in practice—and there are some recommended titles listed at the back of this book. In the meantime, here are four brief tips for leading this new life.

READING THE BIBLE

Throughout this book, I have quoted quite often from the Bible. Christians have always believed that the words of the Bible are the words of God. They believe this because Jesus did, and now they are following him as their Master.

The sooner you get to know what God is saying to you in the Bible, the better. I would begin with Matthew's Gospel, and read the New Testament first. As you read, ask questions like:

- What does this tell me about Jesus?
- What does it tell me about myself?
- How does this challenge me to change my thinking and my life?

Don't worry in the initial stages if you don't understand everything. Stick with it. If you don't have a Bible, get one in modern English. There are many good versions available in Christian bookshops.

SAYING YOUR PRAYERS

One of the joys of turning back to God, being forgiven by him, and being at peace with him, is that he longs to hear the prayers of his children. Try to set aside a time each day when you can talk to God, just like you would to any friend. Share the good times and the bad times of each day. Thank him for his kindness to you. Ask for help to live a life that pleases him. Pray for others who do not know him, that they will come to know him as you have.

GOING TO CHURCH

If church has not been on your agenda, now would be a good time to start again. Look for a church where the Bible is believed and taught as the word of God. Sadly, this is not every church. If you were given this book by a friend, you might try going to church with them. If you don't know of a good church, contact the publishers of this book for more information.

TELLING OTHERS ABOUT JESUS

Everyone needs to know about the wonderful life that awaits us with Christ in the new creation. I am sure that you will have friends and relatives who don't know about Jesus. If it seems appropriate, tell them what has happened to you. They may like to read this book. The church you attend will be delighted to train you to become more skilful at doing this.

Have a great time making the most of the rest of your life!

Matthias Media is an independent Christian publishing company based in Sydney, Australia. To browse our online catalogue, access samples and free downloads, and find more information about our resources, visit our website:

www.matthiasmedia.com.au

How to purchase our resources

1. Through a range of outlets in various parts of the world: visit **www.matthiasmedia.com.au/international.php** for details about recommended retailers in your part of the world.

2. Direct from us over the internet:
   – in the US: www.matthiasmedia.com
   – in Australia and the rest of the world: www.matthiasmedia.com.au

3. Direct from us by phone:
   – in Australia: 1800 814 360 (Sydney: 9663 1478)
   – in the US: 1 866 407 4530
   – international: +61 2 9663 1478

4. Trade enquiries:
   – in the US: sales@matthiasmedia.com
   – in Australia and the rest of the world: sales@matthiasmedia.com.au

Also by John Chapman

A Sinner's Guide to Holiness

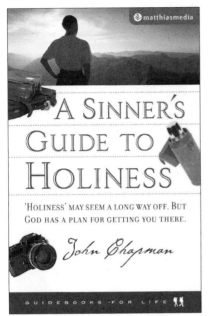

What is holiness? Why do I need it? And why is it such a struggle for me to achieve holiness in my everyday life?

In *A Sinner's Guide to Holiness*, well-known evangelist John Chapman explores what the Bible has to say about holiness—where it begins, how it makes progress in our lives, and its ultimate fulfilment as we are changed into Christ's glorious likeness on the Last Day.

This book is a timely publication in this day and age, when we have often lost sight of the holiness of God. And when we do, it seems like an impossible task to achieve our own holiness. But 'Chappo' tells us that becoming holy is a vital, worthwhile goal for every Christian—even though the first 60 years may be the hardest!

This is the first title in a new series from Matthias Media: Guidebooks for Life. As the series unfolds, it will deal with the important nuts-and-bolts topics that Christians need to know about as we walk each day with our Master.

Read the first book in this new series, and rediscover the joy of being a sinner on the path of holiness.

FOR MORE INFORMATION OR TO ORDER CONTACT:

Matthias Media
Telephone: +61-2-9663-1478
Facsimile: +61-2-9663-3265
Email: sales@matthiasmedia.com.au
www.matthiasmedia.com.au

Matthias Media (USA)
Telephone: 1-866-407-4530
Facsimile: 724-498-1658
Email: sales@matthiasmedia.com
www.matthiasmedia.com